Dr X's Top 10 Villains

Contents

Andrea Smith

Character illustrations by Jon Stuart

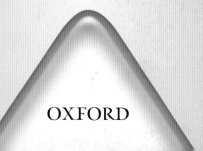

OXFORD

Welcome! My name is Dr X and I am going to take you to meet my favourite, most despicable villains from film, television, books and comics. I hope you're feeling brave …

10 Darth Vader

Look at this photo and then close your eyes. Can you hear that breathing? Can you hear that music? Can you feel the awesome power of the Dark Side?

Villain Profile

Species:	Human (with cyborg implants)
Birthplace:	The planet Tatooine
Real Name:	Anakin Skywalker
Other names:	Lord Vader Dark Lord of the Sith
Base:	Death Star Battle Station
Mission:	To destroy the Jedi Knights and return the Empire to the Dark Side
Strengths:	The power of The Force The skills of a Jedi
Weaknesses:	Pride, family ties

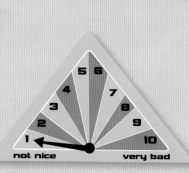

Darth Vader is a famous movie villain. He is masked, mysterious and scary. But in the end, he said sorry ... so he only gets a 1 on my bad-o-meter!

not nice   very bad

3

Vader's story

As a young child, Anakin Skywalker had the strength and skill of a powerful Force shared only by a chosen few – the Jedi. The Jedi were good people who protected peace and justice throughout the galaxy against the evil forces of the Sith. The Sith were rogue Jedi who used their powers to destroy other worlds.

Anakin Skywalker was a brash and rebellious boy. The Sith persuaded him to join them. Anakin turned to the Dark Side.

In a fierce fight with his former master, Obi-Wan Kanobi, Anakin was almost killed. The Sith took his severely burned body and rebuilt it using cyborg implants. His new look was completed by a horrible mask. He became Darth Vader.

Luke Skywalker finally meets his father.

Darth Vader used his skills and powers against the Jedi and he fought many battles with them. Then he discovered that his Jedi enemy was his own son, Luke Skywalker. He began to have doubts about the Dark Side. In a final battle for power, Darth Vader stood aside to let Luke win. Before he died he took off his mask to reveal his true identity and asked his son to forgive him.

The voice of Vader

Different actors played Darth Vader in the films but the 'voice' of Vader was played by James Earl Jones.

Very special effects

The original *Star Wars* film was released in 1977 – before computer animation and CGI (Computer Generated Images). The amazing action sequences were made using film screens and models. These 'special effects' were created by a company called Industrial Light and Magic. Today, this same company uses modern computer technology to create movies such as *Jurassic Park* and *Pirates of the Caribbean*.

9 Doctor Ivo Eggman

Watch out! This guy may look goofy, but he's clever, cunning and not very nice. Just ask Sonic the Hedgehog.

Villain Profile

Species:	Half-human, half-robot
Birthplace:	Believed to be Earth
Other names:	Dr Robotnik
Base:	Death Egg
Mission:	To capture the Chaos Emeralds
	To take over the universe using the power of Chaos Control
Strengths:	Very clever
	Expert in robotics
Weaknesses:	A big ego
	Prone to tantrums

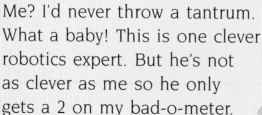

Me? I'd never throw a tantrum. What a baby! This is one clever robotics expert. But he's not as clever as me so he only gets a 2 on my bad-o-meter.

5 6
4 7
3 8
2 9
1 10
not nice   very bad

Eggman of mystery

Very little is known about Doctor Ivo Eggman's past. He changes his appearance all the time and often uses another name – Doctor Robotnik. So he is difficult to track down.

It is thought that, even as a child, Ivo Eggman was fascinated by everything mechanical and robotic. As an adult, his many inventions earned him the title 'Doctor'.

Then, one day, an experiment went wrong. He was blasted with chemicals and turned in to an evil half-human, half-robot. The creature responsible for Doctor Eggman's accident was Sonic the Hedgehog.

Doctor Eggman was determined to get revenge on Sonic. He also wanted to find the Chaos Emeralds that would help him take over the world. He used his scientific genius to create some amazing machines and robots. Many of his robots look like him.

The video game *Sonic the Hedgehog* was first released in 1991. Since then, Sonic has become one of the most recognized video game characters in the world.

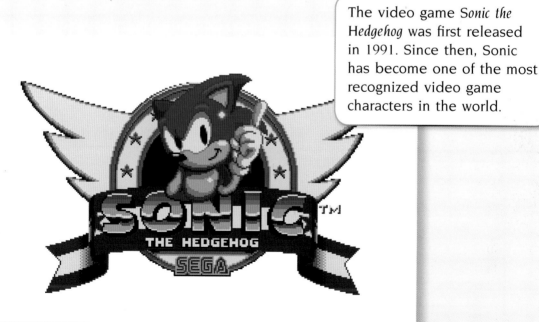

Console wars

Can you imagine a world without computer games? It's hard to believe that only 30 years ago – probably when your parents were children – very few children had computers or computer games.

Early computer games were very basic, but they were great fun to play. Then, games consoles were developed and the games got better and better.

Competition between the makers of different consoles was fierce. The most famous rivalry was between the Sega Megadrive and the Super Nintendo Entertainment System (or SNES for short).

Early computer games like this one had simple graphics.

At first the SNES was most popular. Then the game *Sonic the Hedgehog* was launched for the Sega Megadrive … and sales boomed!

Things change quickly in the world of computer games. Today, Sega is less popular and Nintendo has new competition from the Playstation and X-Box. Who knows what will come next?

Which is your favourite console?			
Sony	**Sega**	**Microsoft**	**Nintendo**
	Sega Megadrive		SNES
Playstation	Sega Saturn		Nintendo 64
Playstation 2	Sega Dreamcast	X-box	Nintendo Game Cube
Playstation 3		X-box 360	Nintendo Wii
PSP			Nintendo DS

8 Count Olaf

Do not read this …
This is not for NICE people …
You have been warned!

Villain Profile

Species:	Human (just about)
Birthplace:	Unknown
Other names:	Too many to mention but they include: Al Funcoot Coach Gengis Captain Julio Sham
Base:	Anywhere close to the Baudelaire children
Mission:	To steal the Baudelaire fortune
Strengths:	Determined Downright mean
Weaknesses:	Greedy Reckless

This is one nasty villain. But I think my eyebrows are better! So he only gets a 3 on my bad-o-meter.

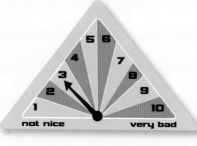

A nasty piece of work

Count Olaf is an actor, heart-throb and super dad. At least, this is how Count Olaf likes to think of himself. Others might disagree.

Olaf claims to be a distant relative of the Baudelaire children: Violet, Klaus and Sunny. After the tragic death of their parents in a fire, the three young Baudelaire orphans are taken in by Count Olaf. The children soon realize that the Count is not a relative. He is just after the fortune left to them by their parents.

The Count will stop at nothing to get his hands on the loot. He even tries to marry Violet during a play when they are supposed to be acting.

Even with his huge eyebrows, Count Olaf is a master of disguise. He has many identities and follows the children wherever they go. He manages to fool nearly everyone … except the Baudelaire children.

The Baudelaire children with the Count from the film A *Series of Unfortunate Events*.

Count Olaf's creator

The books in which Count Olaf appears are part of a series called A *Series of Unfortunate Events*. There are 13 books in this series. The first book is called *The Bad Beginning* and the last book is called *The End*. The author of the books is called Lemony Snicket … or is he?

The real name of the author is Daniel Handler. He lives in San Francisco in the USA. He writes books for adults, too, but uses the pen name Lemony Snicket when he writes for children.

Daniel Handler aka Lemony Snicket.

Count Olaf features in all 13 books in Lemony Snicket's series A *Series of Unfortunate Events*. Read them at your peril!

From page to screen

Many popular children's books have been turned in to films. A film was made of A *Series of Unfortunate Events* in 2004.

Have you seen the films of any of these famous children's books?

- *Watership Down*
- *The Lion the Witch and the Wardrobe*
- *Harry Potter and the Chamber of Secrets*
- *The Golden Compass*
- *Stormbreaker*

7 Davros

So, you think this shrivelled up mutant couldn't possibly be dangerous? Well, think again! This is one scary, hide-behind-the-sofa villain.

Villain Profile

Species:	Kaled
Home planet:	Skaro
Other names:	Dalek Emperor
Base:	Elite Scientific Division, Skaro
Mission:	To become supreme being, ruler of the Universe
Strengths:	Super intelligence Brilliant scientist
Weaknesses:	Arrogant Obsessed

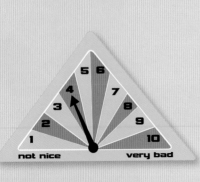

not nice   very bad

Davros is a horrible hero of mine. He did amazing things with technology and created a whole army of baddies to fight a man called Dr Who. (What sort of stupid name is that?) He gets a 4 on my bad-o-meter.

From Kaled to Dalek

The people of the planet Skaro were horribly crippled in a nuclear war. The Kaleds began to mutate. They turned into creatures that were nothing more than brains with tentacles.

Although horribly scarred himself, Davros was a scientific genius. He was an expert in robotics, chemistry, cloning and biology. He made himself a robotic eye and a mobile life-support chair so that he could continue his work.

DALEKS — PETER CUSHING *starring* BERNARD CRIBBINS · RAY BROOKS · JILL CURZON · ROBERTA TOVEY · ANDREW KEIR

INVASION EARTH

TECHNICOLOR
TECHNISCOPE

Davros appeared in the popular science-fiction TV series *Doctor Who* in the 1970s.

Davros took the damaged Kaleds and turned them into an army of mutant robots. He set their brains inside machines that could move. He removed all feelings of weakness from their brains and programmed them for one mission: to exterminate! He called his creations the Daleks.

Davros and the Daleks fought many battles against their arch-enemy Doctor Who.

Doctor Who facts

- *Doctor Who* is listed in the *Guinness Book of World Records* as the longest-running science fiction TV show ever.
- There have been more than 700 episodes of *Doctor Who*. The first episode was broadcast on November 23, 1963.
- So far, 11 different actors have played Dr Who.
- Dr Who travels through time in a police box called the TARDIS. TARDIS stands for *Time And Relative Dimension In Space*.

The War of the Worlds

In 1898, H. G. Wells wrote one of the first science-fiction novels called *The War of the Worlds*. It is about an invasion of Earth by aliens from Mars. On 30th October, 1938, a radio drama based on the novel was broadcast in America. It was presented as a series of news bulletins – which made some people believe that an actual alien invasion was happening! This led to mass panic with some people even fleeing their homes.

This may sound a bit daft today, but in 1938 people still relied on radio to find out what was going on in the world. And H. G. Wells' story was very convincing ...

6 Dr Octopus

This villain is a bit of a handful. He has 6 arms – 4 of them mechanical!

Villain Profile

Species:	Human (with mechanical upgrades)
Birthplace:	New York
Other names:	Dr Otto Octavius
	Doc Ock
Base:	Various (laboratories, warehouses, an abandoned tunnel)
Mission:	To defeat his enemy Spider-Man
	To carry out atomic experiments
Strengths:	Master planner
	Brilliant engineer
	Multiple, powerful arms
Weaknesses:	Unpredictable

Another Doctor ... maybe I can learn a thing or two from him? He gets a 5 on my bad-o-meter.

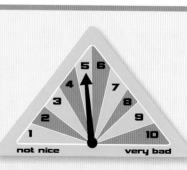

not nice   very bad

Many hands make light work!

Once a brilliant and respected scientist, Dr Otto Octavius designed four mechanical arms to help him with atomic experiments. When an experiment went wrong, he became fused with the arms. His brilliant mind was warped in to that of a mad criminal. He became the arch enemy of that annoying kid who can climb walls – Spider-Man.

Dr Octopus has amazing powers of movement. His four mechanical arms are made from titanium-steel and are capable of lifting huge weights. He can also perform many different tasks at the same time, such as stirring coffee, scratching his head or constructing a machine.

Marvel Comics

Dr Octopus first appeared in the Marvel comic *Amazing Spider-Man 3* in 1963. He has also featured in Spider-Man cartoons, in films and on video games.

Stan Lee.

Stan Lee is one of the creators of Dr Octopus and a former editor of Marvel Comics. Together with his colleagues, Steve Ditko, Jack Kirby and others, they have created many famous comic characters such as: the Hulk, the X-Men, the Fantastic Four, Captain America, Daredevil, Ghost Rider and Iron Man.

Which comic characters can you spot in this picture?

5 The White Witch

This is one powerful lady who held a whole world in a wintery spell for 100 years. Oh, and she can also turn people to stone – which is pretty scary!

Villain Profile

Species:	Human
Other names:	Her Imperial Majesty Jadis
	Queen of Narnia
	Chatelaine of Cair Paravel,
	Empress of the Lone Islands
Base:	The Witch's Castle
Mission:	To rule Narnia
	To defeat Aslan
Strengths:	Cunning
	Turning people into stone
	Making Turkish delight
Weaknesses:	Quick temper
	Fear of lions
	Ancient prophecies

not nice   very bad

The white witch is bothered by four kids – just like me. And she likes Turkish delight. She definitely deserves a 6 on my bad-o-meter.

The Lion, the Witch and the Wardrobe

The White Witch is one cool storybook villain. She was created by the writer C. S. Lewis and appears in a number of his novels. The most famous of these is *The Lion, the Witch and the Wardrobe*. In this story, she has taken over the land of Narnia and has magically forced the country into an endless, icy winter.

There is only one thing that can stop her. According to an ancient prophecy: "When two sons of Adam and two daughters of Eve (two boys and two girls) fill the four thrones at Cair Paravel, the reign of the White Witch will end".

The Lion, the Witch and the Wardrobe was first published in 1950. It is still popular today.

So when four children – Peter, Susan, Edmund and Lucy – find their way into Narnia through a magical wardrobe, the White Witch has to use all her cunning to try and capture them.

Edmund, Lucy, Susan and Peter.

19

Other female baddies

Here are some other tough ladies that you might want to watch out for …

Watch out for this woman's claws! This is **Catwoman**. She was originally created by Bill Finger and Bob Kane at DC Comics and is one of Batman's enemies. Clever and agile with a taste for high class robberies, she knows how to make the giant bat flap.

In his book, *The Witches*, the writer Roald Dahl created the character **The Grand High Witch**. In the story she comes up with a plan for getting rid of all the children in England. She takes over all the sweet shops and sells poisoned sweets that will turn children into mice!

He may sound like fun, but this evil villain is no barrel of laughs …

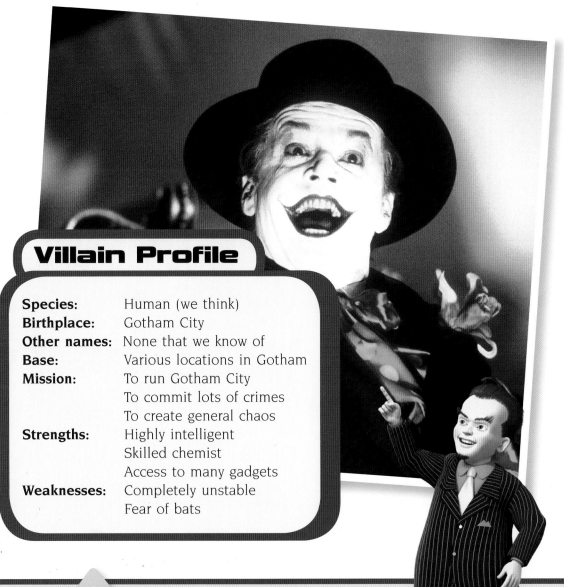

Villain Profile

Species:	Human (we think)
Birthplace:	Gotham City
Other names:	None that we know of
Base:	Various locations in Gotham
Mission:	To run Gotham City
	To commit lots of crimes
	To create general chaos
Strengths:	Highly intelligent
	Skilled chemist
	Access to many gadgets
Weaknesses:	Completely unstable
	Fear of bats

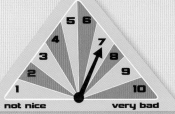

5 6
4 7
3 8
2 9
1 10
not nice   very bad

This guy is such a snappy dresser that he gets a 7 on my bad-o-meter.

The joke's on you!

One day, whilst crime-fighting in Gotham City, Batman pushed a petty thief into a vat of acid. The man escaped but his face was disfigured into a horrible grin. He became the Joker – an insane criminal mastermind bent on revenge against Batman.

The Joker spends his time inventing lots of evil, horrible gadgets. His particular favourite is *Joker Venom* – a fatal toxin that sends its victims into fits of laughter. It locks their faces into a permanent grin.

The Joker appears in the comic books published by DC Comics. He first appeared in *Batman* 1 Spring 1940. He was created by Bill Finger, Bob Kane and Jerry Robinson.

Snappy dressers

The Joker dresses well but if you're looking for villains with true style, check these guys out …

Dracula is always a well turned out gent. But don't get too close – he has a nasty bite!

If white is your colour, check out **Saruman.** He is the evil wizard from the book *The Lord of the Rings*.

If tights are more your thing, look at the **Sheriff of Nottingham** and **Guy of Gisbourne** for style. They are the impeccably dressed enemies of Robin Hood.

He's back. He's bad. He's the one and only … *Shhhhh* – don't say it!

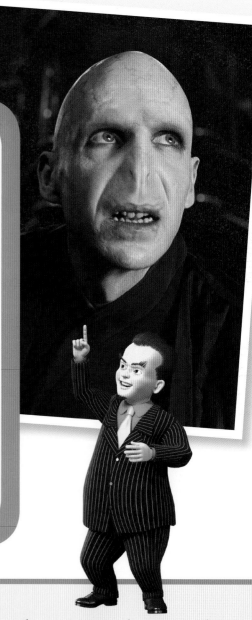

Villain Profile

Species:	Half-blood (Half human/half wizard)
Birthplace:	Orphanage in London
Other names:	Lord Voldemort
	You-Know-Who
	The Dark Lord
	Tom Marvolo Riddle
Base:	Various – but has been seen in the Forbidden Forest and in the back of Professor Quirrell's head
Mission:	To become all powerful again and rule the wizarding world
	To destroy Harry Potter
Strengths:	Cunning and ruthless
	Can perform powerful magic – like the Horcrux curse
Weaknesses:	Harry Potter

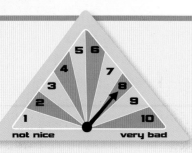

5 6
4 7
3 8
2 9
1 10
not nice   very bad

You-Know-Who is certainly one evil character. But I prefer a more scientific approach to world domination. He gets an 8 on my bad-o-meter.

The Dark Lord

Lord Voldemort (oops, I said it!) is the arch enemy of Harry Potter. He-who-must-not-be-named is evil in its purist form.

Lord Voldemort was the son of the witch Merope Gaunt and the muggle (human) Tom Riddle. When her husband found out Merope was a witch, he abandoned her. He didn't know she was expecting his child.

Merope died shortly after giving birth to her son. She survived long enough to give him the name Tom Marvolo Riddle, after his father and his grandfather.

Tom Marvolo Riddle grew up in an orphanage but was determined to defy his humble origins. He would eventually transform himself into the most powerful and most feared wizard of all time.

Ron, Harry and Hermione.

The Harry Potter phenomenon

In 1995, J. K. Rowling was an unknown, struggling writer trying to get her first book published. Now she is one of the most successful children's authors ever. Some say she is richer than the Queen!

The Harry Potter series has sold millions and millions of copies worldwide. But why are her books so appealing?

Here are some of the reasons …
- great plots
- believable characters
- plenty of action
- interesting settings
- really great baddies
- exciting games – like Quidditch.

Can you think of any others?

These are the 7 books in the Harry Potter series. Some words have magically disappeared – do you know what the missing words are?
1. Harry Potter and the X Stone
2. Harry Potter and the Chamber of X
3. Harry Potter and the Prisoner of X
4. Harry Potter and the X of Fire
5. Harry Potter and the X of the Phoenix
6. Harry Potter and the Half-Blood X
7. Harry Potter and the Deathly X

2 Lex Luthor

Rich, handsome and powerful, this is one villain with almost as much style as me ...

Villain Profile

Species:	Human
Birthplace:	Metropolis
Other names:	Alexander "Lex" Joseph Luthor
Base:	Big flashy office in Metropolis
Mission:	To commit lots of crimes To be famous To be fabulously wealthy
Strengths:	Super intelligent Cunning
Weaknesses:	Lois Lane

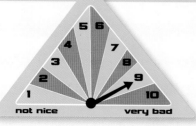

not nice very bad

Anyone who dedicates his life to defeating Superman is a hero in my book! He gets a 9 on my bad-o-meter.

Another great scientist . . .

The original comic book Lex Luthor was a mad scientist who plots to take over the world using fantastic machines. In his youth, he had few friends except Superboy. Then, one day, Superboy causes an accident in Lex's laboratory. (Have you noticed how many villains are created in this way?) Lex's hair falls out and he vows revenge on Superboy … who later becomes Superman.

More recently, Lex Luthor has evolved into a modern criminal mastermind. People think he is a respectable businessman. He is sometimes suspected of crimes and is often arrested and sent to prison. But Lex always manages to escape to continue his criminal activities and his battle with Superman.

Lex Luthor is a DC Comics super villain created by Jerry Siegel and Joe Shuster.

Lex Luthor first appeared in *Action Comics* 23 in 1940. Since then he has appeared in films, on television, in video games and in novels.

Christopher Reeve ...
a real Superman

Christopher Reeve was born on 25th September, 1952, in New York City. He grew up with his mother, step father and brother in Princeton, New Jersey. After graduating from high school, Reeve studied at New York's famous Juilliard School of Performing Arts. He is best known for playing Superman but he also played many other roles.

Reeve was a very fit and sporty person. He enjoyed sailing, scuba diving, skiing, cycling, gliding, mountain climbing and horse riding. He often competed in horse-riding events.

Christopher Reeve in his most famous role as Superman.

On 27th May, 1995, Reeve fell from his horse, Buck. The accident left him paralyzed from the neck down. Despite his severe disability, he continued to lead the life of a super hero. He spent much of his time raising money for spinal injury charities and campaigning for medical research. He died very suddenly in 2004.

1 Magneto

This genius of genetics certainly has a magnetic personality ...

Villain Profile

Species:	Mutant human
Birthplace:	Unknown
Other names:	The Creator
	Eric Magnus
	Michael Xavier
	White Pilgrim
Base:	Unknown
Mission:	To destroy all humans and create a world of mutants
Strengths:	Can control all forms of magnetism
	Can manipulate: energy, visible light, radio waves, ultraviolet light, gamma rays, and x-rays
Weaknesses:	Getting injured

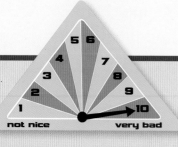

not nice   very bad

This guy is as bad as they come. He gets a perfect 10 on my bad-o-meter.

The pull of power

Magneto is an expert on genetic manipulation – that means changing human beings to give them different, often superhuman, powers. He has even managed to create clones and artificial intelligence.

Magneto's own superpowers include the ability to control magnetic forces. He can erect a magnetic force field around himself for protection, or assemble a complicated machine within seconds. He has designed many magnetically powered vehicles, spacecraft, robots and computers.

As a young man Magneto met Charles Xavier. Both were mutants with superhuman powers and they became friends. But Magneto had evil ambitions to create a race of super-mutants that would take over the world. Charles Xavier wanted humans and mutants to live in harmony. Charles and his mutant warriors – known as the X-Men – do battle with Magneto and his Brotherhood in order to protect human kind.

Magneto first appeared in the Marvel Comic X-Men 1 in 1963 and has appeared more recently in three X-Men films.

Genetic modification

All living things contain *genes*. Genes are the instructions that tell each living thing how to grow, what to look like and how to behave. If you change these genes, you can change the way a living thing develops.

Scientists have found ways to change certain genes in plants and animals. They want to 'genetically modify' some plants and animals that we use for food by changing their genes. With more and more people on the planet, producing enough food to feed us all is a challenge. Some scientists think genetic modification (or GM) can help. Others disagree.

Arguments for GM	Arguments against GM
• GM can create food crops or animals that are resistant to disease. • GM creates food crops or animals that grow bigger and faster than normal plants and animals. • GM creates food crops that last longer and don't rot.	• The properties of GM plants will spread to other plants – including weeds. This could mean bigger weeds that are resistant to diseases or chemicals. • GM plants will be resistant to insects. This means that many insects – and the birds and other animals that feed on them – will die. • Animals that are genetically modified to grow bigger may suffer. • No one knows how 'safe' it is to eat living things that have been genetically modified.

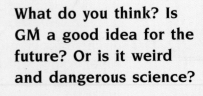

What do you think? Is GM a good idea for the future? Or is it weird and dangerous science?